Ruby Bridges
—— GOES ——
TO SCHOOL
My True Story

• By Ruby Bridges •

ISBN-13: 978-0-545-10855-3
ISBN-10: 0-545-10855-1

40 39 38   19/0

Printed in the U.S.A.   40
First printing, September 2009

Ruby Bridges
— GOES —
TO SCHOOL
MY TRUE STORY

• BY RUBY BRIDGES •

SCHOLASTIC INC.

A long time ago,
some people thought that black people
and white people should not be friends.

In some places,
black people were not allowed
to live in the same neighborhoods
as white people.

In some places,
black people were not allowed
to eat in the same restaurants
as white people.

And in some places,
black children and white children
could not go to the same schools.
This is called segregation.

The United States government said:
"Segregation is wrong."
People should live
where they want.
People should eat
where they want.
Children should go to school
where they want.

My name is Ruby Bridges.
In 1960,
I went to kindergarten
in a school for black children.
I liked my school.
I liked my teacher.
I liked my friends.

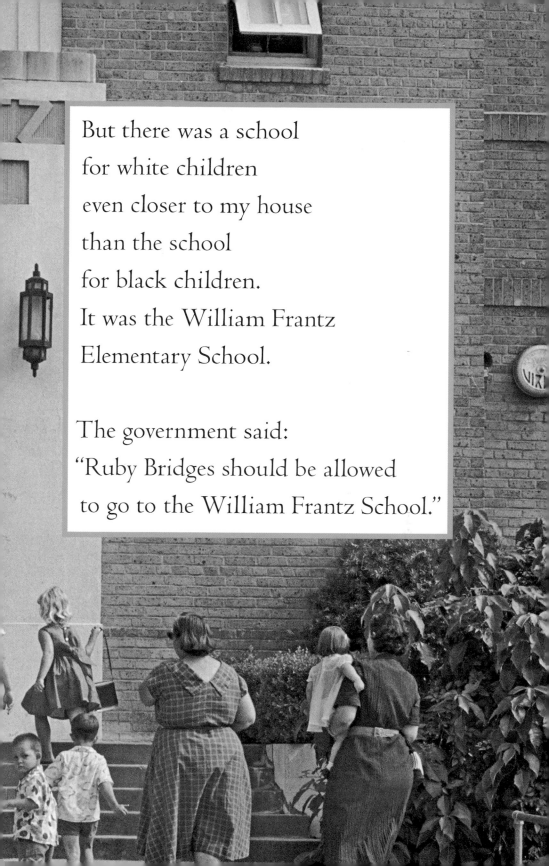

But there was a school
for white children
even closer to my house
than the school
for black children.
It was the William Frantz
Elementary School.

The government said:
"Ruby Bridges should be allowed
to go to the William Frantz School."

In 1961, I was in first grade.
My mother took me
to the Frantz School.
Marshals came with us
to make sure that we were safe.

Some people did not want a black child
to go to the white school.

They stood near the school.
They yelled at me to go away.

Parents took their children
out of the school.
I was alone with my teacher,
Mrs. Henry.

I loved Mrs. Henry.
And Mrs. Henry loved me.
I was a very good student.
I learned math.
I learned how to read.
But I wished the children
would come back.

Months and months passed.
Then one day, children began
to come back to school.

At last,
I had friends to play with!
I was very, very happy!

Many people have read about me
in newspapers and books.

A famous writer, John Steinbeck,
wrote about me. He wrote that
I was very brave.

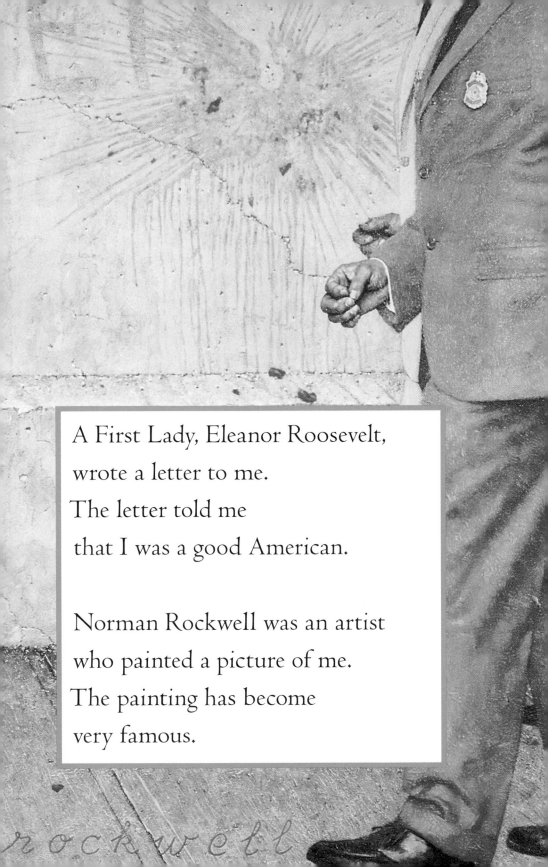

A First Lady, Eleanor Roosevelt,
wrote a letter to me.
The letter told me
that I was a good American.

Norman Rockwell was an artist
who painted a picture of me.
The painting has become
very famous.

Now I am grown up.
I am married.
I have children.

One day,
Mrs. Henry and I
were both asked to be
on a TV show.
That was the first time
we had seen each other
in many years.
Now we talk to each other often.

Now black children and white children
can go to the same schools.
I like to visit schools.
I tell my story to children.